130906

Carl Nielsen

FANTASY PIECES

opus 2

for
Oboe and Piano

Score (Piano Part)

THE CARL NIELSEN EDITION

THE ROYAL LIBRARY

COPENHAGEN

DISTRIBUTION:

EDITION WILHELM HANSEN

FANTASY PIECES
FOR OBOE AND PIANO

FANTASISTYKKER
FOR OBO OG KLAVER

1.

ROMANCE
ROMANCE

Op. 2

Andante con duolo

Oboe

Carl Nielsen

FANTASY PIECES

opus 2

for
Oboe and Piano

THE CARL NIELSEN EDITION
THE ROYAL LIBRARY
COPENHAGEN

DISTRIBUTION :
EDITION WILHELM HANSEN

FANTASY PIECES
FOR OBOE AND PIANO

FANTASISTYKKER
FOR OBO OG KLAVER

1.

ROMANCE
ROMANCE
Andante con duolo

Carl Nielsen
Op. 2

2.

HUMORESQUE
HUMORESQUE
Allegretto scherzando

Oboe

HUMORESQUE

2.

HUMORESQUE

Allegretto scherzando